LOVE

Quotations from the Heart

RUNNING PRESS

PHILADELPHIA • LONDON

INTRODUCTION

Love is the most personal of emotions. It is our reason for being, and our reason for staying.

Each of us feels love and expresses love differently; everyone in love is unique, and every pair of lovers creates a singular world. Yet all lovers share the courage to be in love. A loving relationship is the delicate merger of two souls. There's risk in that, but there's no more powerful magic in all the universe. Even time can't break bonds forged of love.

The quotations in this book are the words of men and women who have been in love—from Euripides to Eleanor

Roosevelt, and from Robert Burns to David Byrne. These individuals, made famous by their other achievements, succinctly express their feelings about their more intimate glory. Here are centuries of thought on the eternal topic of love: how it feels to fall in love, how love hurts, and how it heals.

Of course, anyone can become an expert on love: one just has to be in love.

THE LOVING

are the daring.

BAYARD TAYLOR
(1825–1878)
American writer

ALL LOVE

is sweet,

Given or returned.

PERCY BYSSHE SHELLEY
(1792–1822)
English poet

THERE IS ONLY

one happiness in life,

to love and be loved.

GEORGE SAND
(1804–1876)
French writer

THE GIVING OF LOVE

is an education in itself.

ELEANOR ROOSEVELT
(1884–1962)
American first lady

LOVE MUST BE LEARNED,

and learned again and again;

there is no end to it.

KATHERINE ANN PORTER
(1890–1980)
American writer

PAINS OF LOVE

be sweeter far

Than all other

pleasures are.

JOHN DRYDEN
(1631–1700)
English poet

ONE MUST LEARN

to love, and go through a

good deal of suffering to get

to it . . . and the journey is

always towards the other

soul . . . .

D.H. LAWRENCE
(1885–1930)
English writer

TO LOVE

is to place our happiness

in the happiness of another.

GOTTFRIED WILHELM von LEIBNIZ
(1646–1716)
German philosopher and
mathematician

LOVE MAKES UP
for the lack of long memories
by a sort of magic.
All other affections need a
past: love creates a past
which envelops us,
as if by enchantment.

BENJAMIN CONSTANT
DE REBECQUE
(1767–1830)
French writer and politician

THERE IS

but one genuine

love-potion—consideration.

MENANDER
(342–292 B.C.)
Greek playwright

GRATITUDE

looks to the past

and love to the present . . . .

C.S. LEWIS
(1898–1963)
English writer

LIFE HAS

taught us that love does not

consist in gazing at each

other but in looking

outward together

in the same direction.

ANTOINE DE SAINT–EXUPÉRY
(1900–1944)
French writer and aviator

LOVE ALONE

is capable of uniting

living beings in such a way as

to complete and fulfill them,

for it alone takes them and

joins them by what is deepest

in themselves.

PIERRE TEILHARD DE CHARDIN
(1881–1955)
French paleontologist
and philosopher

HARMONY

is pure love,

for love is complete

agreement.

LOPE DE VEGA
(1562–1635)
Spanish writer

LOVE IS

but the discovery of ourselves

in others, and the delight in

the recognition.

ALEXANDER SMITH
(1830–1867)
Scottish poet

THE ONLY TRUE GIFT

is a portion of yourself.

RALPH WALDO EMERSON
(1803–1882)
American writer

LOVE

is all we have,

the only way that

each can help the other.

EURIPIDES
(480–405 B.C.)
Greek playwright

...WHAT I DO

And what I dream

include thee, as the wine

Must taste of its own grapes.

ELIZABETH BARRETT BROWNING
(1806–1861)
English poet

MY LOVE

for you is mixed

throughout my body. . . .

ANCIENT EGYPTIAN LOVE SONG
(c. 1550–1080 B.C.)

GROW OLD ALONG WITH ME!

The best is yet to be,

The last of life

for which the first was made.

ROBERT BROWNING
(1812–1889)
English poet

I LOVE THEE

with the breath,

Smiles, tears, of all my life!

ELIZABETH BARRETT BROWNING
(1806–1861)
English poet

BUT TO SEE HER

was to love her,

Love but her,

and love her for ever.

ROBERT BURNS
(1759–1796)
Scottish poet

COME LIVE
with me, and be my love,
And we will
some new pleasures prove,
Of golden sands,
and crystal brooks,
With silken lines,
and silver hooks.

JOHN DONNE
(1572–1631)
English poet

THE WAY TO LOVE ANYTHING

is to realize that it might be lost.

G.K. CHESTERTON
(1874–1936)
English writer

TO FEAR LOVE

is to fear life....

BERTRAND RUSSELL
(1872–1970)
English mathematician
and philosopher

ANY TIME

that is not spent on love

is wasted.

TORQUATO TASSO
(1544–1595)
Italian poet

OH LOVE,

as long as you can love.

FERDINAND FREILIGRATH
(1810–1876)
German poet

THE GREAT

tragedy of life

is not that men perish,

but that they cease to love.

W. SOMERSET MAUGHAM
(1874–1965)
English writer

LOVE IS...

born with the pleasure of
looking at each other, it is fed
with the necessity of seeing
each other, it is concluded
with the impossibility of
separation!

JOSÉ MARTÍ Y PERÉZ
(1853–1895)
Cuban writer

IN LOVE,

everything is true,

everything is false;

it is the one subject on which

one cannot express

an absurdity.

NICHOLAS CHAMFORT
(1741–1794)
French writer

THE BEST PROOF

of love is trust.

DR. JOYCE BROTHERS, b. 1928
American writer and lecturer

BETWEEN WHOM

there is hearty truth

there is love . . . .

HENRY DAVID THOREAU
(1817–1862)
American writer

LOVE IS

the only game

that is not called

on account of darkness.

ANONYMOUS

LOVE IS THE

triumph of imagination

over intelligence.

H.L. MENCKEN
(1880–1956)
American writer

OH, LIFE IS A

glorious cycle of song,

A medley of extemporanea;

And love is a thing that

can never go wrong;

And I am Marie of Roumania.

DOROTHY PARKER
(1893–1967)
American writer

LOVE

begets love.

This torment is my joy.

THEODORE ROETHKE
(1908–1963)
American poet

THE COURSE

of true love

never did run smooth.

WILLIAM SHAKESPEARE
(1564–1616)
English dramatist and poet

WHEN

love and skill

work together,

expect a masterpiece.

JOHN RUSKIN
(1819–1900)
English writer

THERE IS

only one kind of love,

but there are a thousand

different versions.

LA ROCHEFOUCAULD
(1613–1680)
French moralist

LOVE

and the gentle heart

are but a single thing.

DANTE ALIGHIERI
(1265–1321)
Italian poet

LOVE DISTILLS

desire upon the eyes,

love brings bewitching grace

into the heart....

EURIPIDES
(c. 484–406 B.C.)
Greek playwright

IN MANY WAYS

doth the full heart reveal

The presence of love

it would conceal.

SAMUEL TAYLOR COLERIDGE
(1772–1824)
English writer

GIVE ALL TO LOVE;

Obey thy heart . . . .

RALPH WALDO EMERSON
(1803–1882)
American writer

HEARTS ARE NOT

had as a gift

but hearts are earned....

WILLIAM BUTLER YEATS
(1865–1939)
Irish poet and dramatist

LOVE IS,

above all, the gift of oneself.

JEAN ANOUILH
(1910–1987)
French playwright

THERE IS ALWAYS

something left to love.

And if you ain't learned that,

you ain't learned nothing.

LORRAINE HANSBERRY
(1930–1965)
American playwright

FOR ONE HUMAN
being to love another: that is
perhaps the most difficult of
all our tasks, the ultimate,
the last test and proof, the
work for which all other
work is but preparation.

RAINER MARIA RILKE
(1875–1926)
German poet

I HAVE ENJOYED

the happiness of the world;

I have lived and loved.

JOHANN VON SCHILLER
(1759–1805)
German poet

LOVE

is merely

a madness....

WILLIAM SHAKESPEARE
(1564–1616)
English dramatist and poet

TO LOVE DEEPLY

in one direction makes us

more loving in all others.

MADAME SWETCHINE
(1782–1857)
Russian-born French writer

IN LOVE

the paradox occurs that two

beings become one and yet

remain two.

ERICH FROMM
(1900–1980)
American psychoanalyst

HOW VAST

a memory has Love!

ALEXANDER POPE
(1688–1744)
English writer

TO GET THE FULL

value of joy you must have

someone to divide it with.

MARK TWAIN
(1835–1910)
American writer

IMMATURE LOVE

says: "I love you

because I need you."

Mature love says: "I need you

because I love you."

ERICH FROMM
(1900–1980)
American psychoanalyst

HE WHO

is not impatient

is not in love.

ITALIAN PROVERB

LOVE IS SUPREME

and unconditional;

like is nice but limited.

DUKE ELLINGTON
(1899–1974)
American bandleader
and composer

TO LOVE

is to receive a glimpse

of heaven.

KAREN SUNDE, b. 1942
American actor-playwright

TO LOVE

for the sake of being loved

is human; but to love for the

sake of loving is angelic.

ALPHONSE DE LAMARTINE
(1790–1869)
French poet

THE STORY OF

a love is not important—

what is important is that one

is capable of love. It is

perhaps the only glimpse we

are permitted of eternity.

HELEN HAYES, b. 1900
American actress

WINE COMES IN

at the mouth; love comes in

through the eye.

HENRI MATISSE
(1869–1954)
French artist

LOVE

is the greatest refreshment

in life.

PABLO PICASSO
(1881–1973)
Spanish painter

FIRST ROMANCE, first love, is something so special to all of us, both emotionally and physically, that it touches our lives and enriches them forever.

ROSEMARY ROGERS, b. 1932
American writer

WHEN I WAS
very young I fell deeply in
love...and really believed I
would never feel that way
again...then nine years later
...I did, and much, much
more strongly and deeply
than before.

ISAK DINESEN
(1885–1962)
Danish writer

THE PROOF THAT

experience teaches us

nothing is that the end of

one love does not prevent us

from beginning another.

PAUL BOURGET
(1852–1935)
French writer

AMONG THOSE

whom I like or admire, I can

find no common

denominator, but among

those whom I love, I can: all

of them make me laugh.

W.H. AUDEN
(1907–1973)
American poet

SOMETIMES IT'S A form of love just to talk to somebody that you have nothing in common with and still be fascinated by their presence.

DAVID BYRNE, b. 1952
American entertainer

IN LOVE YOU FIND
the oddest combinations:
Materialistic people find
themselves in love with
idealists. Clingers fall in love
with players;...homebodies
capture and try to smother
butterflies. If it weren't so
serious we could laugh at it.

GEORGE DAVIS, b. 1939
American writer and teacher

WE LOVE

the things we love

for what they are.

ROBERT FROST
(1874–1963)
American poet

WE DON'T LOVE

qualities, we love a person;

sometimes by reason of

their defects as well as

their qualities.

JACQUES MARITAIN
(1882–1973)
French philosopher

...IF YOU

love somebody,

tell them.

ROD McKUEN, b. 1933
American poet

LOVE IS...

an endless mystery, for it has

nothing else to explain it.

RABINDRANATH TAGORE
(1861–1941)
Hindu poet

WE FIND REST

in those we love,

and we provide a resting place

in ourselves for those

who love us.

SAINT BERNARD OF CLAIRVAUX
(1090–1153)
French ecclesiastic

I LIKE NOT ONLY

to be loved,

but to be told I am loved.

GEORGE ELIOT
(1819–1880)
English writer

WHEN LOVE IS GOOD

it can make you fly.

Winning it is worth the risk.

People fall in love

and glow for weeks.

GEORGE DAVIS, b. 1939
American writer and teacher

TO LOVE AND WIN

is the best thing;

to love and lose, the next best.

WILLIAM MAKEPEACE THACKERAY
(1811–1863)
English writer

WHERE LOVE REIGNS

the impossible

may be attained.

INDIAN PROVERB

WHEN YOU

love someone

all your saved-up wishes

start coming out.

ELIZABETH BOWEN
(1899–1973)
Irish writer

LOVE

knoweth no laws.

SIR JOHN LYLY
(1554?–1606)
English writer

...THE COURAGE

to share your feelings

is critical to sustaining

a love relationship.

HAROLD H. BLOOMFIELD, b. 1944
American psychiatrist and writer
ROBERT B. KORY, b. 1950
American lecturer

HOW BOLD ONE GETS

when one is sure of

being loved!

SIGMUND FREUD
(1856–1939)
Austrian founder of psychoanalysis

LOVE IS AN ACT

of endless forgiveness,

a tender look

which becomes a habit.

PETER USTINOV, b. 1921
English actor and writer

LOVE IS WHAT

you've been through

with somebody.

JAMES THURBER
(1894–1961)
American writer and cartoonist

TAKE HOLD LIGHTLY;

let go lightly. This is

one of the great secrets

of felicity in love.

SPANISH PROVERB

LOVE IS AN

irresistible desire to be

irresistibly desired.

ROBERT FROST
(1874–1963)
American poet

LOVE CURES PEOPLE—

both the ones who

give it and the ones who

receive it.

DR. KARL MENNINGER, b. 1893
American psychiatrist

WHERE LOVE IS

concerned, too much is not

even enough!

P. A.C. DE BEAUMARCHAIS
(1732–1799)
French playwright

LOVE

conquers all things . . . .

VIRGIL
(70–19 B.C.)
Roman poet